BUGS

GRASSHOPPERS

by Emma Huddleston

Consultant: Beth Gambro
Reading Specialist, Yorkville, Illinois

BEARPORT
PUBLISHING

Minneapolis, Minnesota

Teaching Tips

Before Reading

- Look at the cover of the book. Discuss the picture and the title.

- Ask readers to brainstorm a list of what they already know about grasshoppers. What can they expect to see in the book?

- Go on a picture walk, looking through the pictures to discuss vocabulary and make predictions about the text.

During Reading

- Read for purpose. As they are reading, encourage readers to think about the grasshopper's life and the impacts the bug has on other things.

- If readers encounter an unknown word, ask them to look at the sounds in the word. Then, ask them to look at the rest of the page. Are there any clues to help them understand?

After Reading

- Encourage readers to pick a buddy and reread the book together.

- Ask readers to name three things from the book that grasshoppers do. Go back and find the pages that tell about these things.

- Ask readers to write or draw something that they learned about grasshoppers.

Credits:

Cover and title page, © NEFS/Shutterstock; 3, © GlobalP/ iStock; 5, © Pally/Alamy; 6, © MidoSemsem/Shutterstock; 6, © THP Creative/Shutterstock; 7, © Dopeyden/iStock; 9, © Konstantin39/Shutterstock; 10–11, © Avalon.red/Alamy; 12–13, © Shelly MD Photography/Shutterstock; 15, © Maryna Auramchuk/iStock; 17, © LESSY SEBASTIAN/gettyimages; 18–19, © Brberrys/Shutterstock; 20–21, © lucky vectorstudio/ Shutterstock; 22, © Mang Kelin/Shutterstock, © Miguel Angel RM/Shutterstock, © Silvia Dubois/Shutterstock, © michieldb/ iStock; 23TL, © o0o0o1111/Shutterstock; 23TR, © bruev/ iStock; 23BL, © Lukas Hejtman/Shutterstock; 23BR, © ABDESIGN/iStock.

Library of Congress Cataloging-in-Publication Data

Names: Huddleston, Emma, author.
Title: Grasshoppers / Emma Huddleston.
Description: Bearcub books. | Minneapolis, Minnesota : Bearport Publishing
  Company, [2022] | Series: Bugs | Includes bibliographical references and
  index.
Identifiers: LCCN 2021026726 (print) | LCCN 2021026727 (ebook) | ISBN
  9781636913766 (library binding) | ISBN 9781636913834 (paperback) | ISBN
  9781636913902 (ebook)
Subjects: LCSH: Grasshoppers--Juvenile literature.
Classification: LCC QL508.A2 H85 2022 (print) | LCC QL508.A2 (ebook) |
  DDC 595.7/26--dc23
LC record available at https://lccn.loc.gov/2021026726
LC ebook record available at https://lccn.loc.gov/2021026727

For more information, write to Bearport Publishing, 5357 Penn Avenue South, Minneapolis, MN 55419. Printed in the United States of America.

Contents

A Big Jump

A green grasshopper sits in the sun.

Suddenly, it springs into the air.

Let's learn about this jumping bug!

5

There are many kinds of grasshoppers.

Some are smaller than a coin.

Other grasshoppers can be as big as a bar of soap.

Grasshoppers **crawl** around on long legs.

But they are known best for jumping.

They push off the ground and spring.

Their legs are very strong.

Leg

Grasshoppers open up their wings when they jump.

The wings help them hop far.

Boing!

Wings

Sometimes, grasshoppers fly away to stay safe.

They jump from other animals.

Birds and frogs eat grasshoppers.

Snakes eat them, too.

Their colors can also keep them safe.

Sometimes, the bugs hide.

Green grasshoppers hide on green leaves.

Brown and tan ones are the same color as dirt.

Grasshoppers use two long **feelers** to smell food.

The bugs nibble on leaves.

Sharp **jaws** help them bite hard seeds.

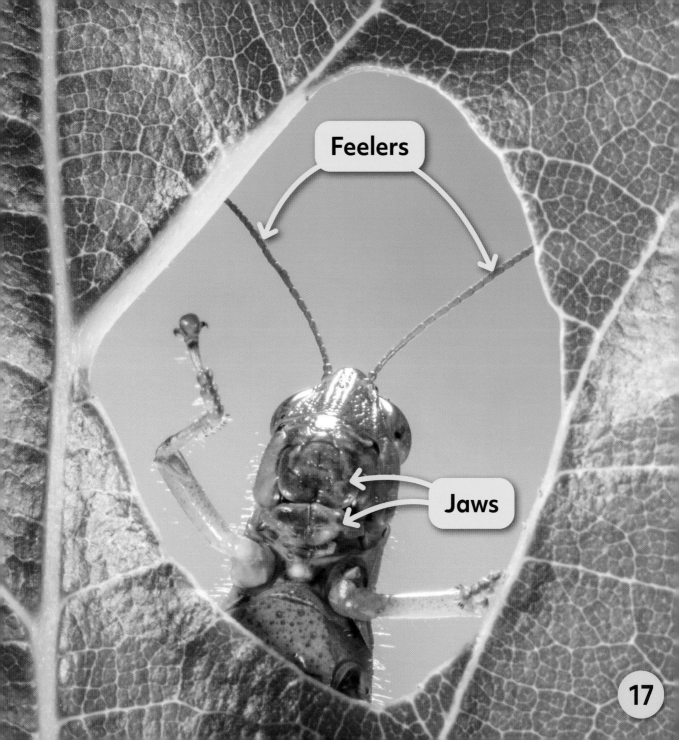

Feelers

Jaws

Most grasshoppers eat only plants.

Sometimes they eat too many.

They may eat **crops** grown for people.

This takes away from our food.

But not all grasshoppers are bad.

Some help farmers!

A few munching grasshoppers keep crops from growing too much.

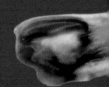

Thank you, jumping bugs!

21

A Grasshopper's Life

Egg

Adult

Young grasshopper

Glossary

crawl to move with the body close to the ground

crops plants grown for food

feelers long, thin body parts that come out of a bug's head

jaws parts in an animal's mouth that help with chewing

Index

Read More

Abraham, Anika. *Grasshoppers (Creepy Crawlers).* New York: Cavendish Square, 2019.

Perish, Patrick. *Grasshoppers (Insects Up Close).* Minneapolis: Bellwether Media, 2018.

Learn More Online

1. Go to **www.factsurfer.com** or scan the QR code below.
2. Enter "**Grasshopper Bug**" into the search box.
3. Click on the cover of this book to see a list of websites.

About the Author

Emma Huddleston lives in the Twin Cities with her husband. She enjoys writing children's books and spending time outside. She often sees the interesting bugs in this series!